WITHDRAWN

CREEPY CRAWLIES

Hissing Cockroaches

by Kari Schuetz

BELLWETHER MEDIA • MINNEAPOLIS, MN

16.95

apple

11/15

Note to Librarians, Teachers, and Parents:

Blastoff! Readers are carefully developed by literacy experts and combine standards-based content with developmentally appropriate text.

Level 1 provides the most support through repetition of high-frequency words, light text, predictable sentence patterns, and strong visual support.

Level 2 offers early readers a bit more challenge through varied simple sentences, increased text load, and less repetition of high-frequency words.

Level 3 advances early-fluent readers toward fluency through increased text and concept load, less reliance on visuals, longer sentences, and more literary language.

Level 4 builds reading stamina by providing more text per page, increased use of punctuation, greater variation in sentence patterns, and increasingly challenging vocabulary.

Level 5 encourages children to move from "learning to read" to "reading to learn" by providing even more text, varied writing styles, and less familiar topics.

Whichever book is right for your reader, Blastoff! Readers are the perfect books to build confidence and encourage a love of reading that will last a lifetime!

This edition first published in 2016 by Bellwether Media, Inc.

No part of this publication may be reproduced in whole or in part without written permission of the publisher. For information regarding permission, write to Bellwether Media, Inc., Attention: Permissions Department, 5357 Penn Avenue South, Minneapolis, MN 55419.

Library of Congress Cataloging-in-Publication Data

Schuetz, Kari.
 Hissing Cockroaches / by Kari Schuetz.
  pages cm. – (Blastoff! Readers. Creepy Crawlies)
Summary: "Developed by literacy experts for students in kindergarten through grade three, this book introduces hissing cockroaches to young readers through leveled text and related photos"– Provided by publisher.
 Audience: Ages 5-8
 Audience: K to grade 3
Includes bibliographical references and index.
 ISBN 978-1-62617-223-4 (hardcover: alk. paper)
1. Madagascar hissing cockroach–Juvenile literature. I. Title.
QL505.7.B4S38 2016
595.7'28–dc23

                          2015002615

Table of **Contents**

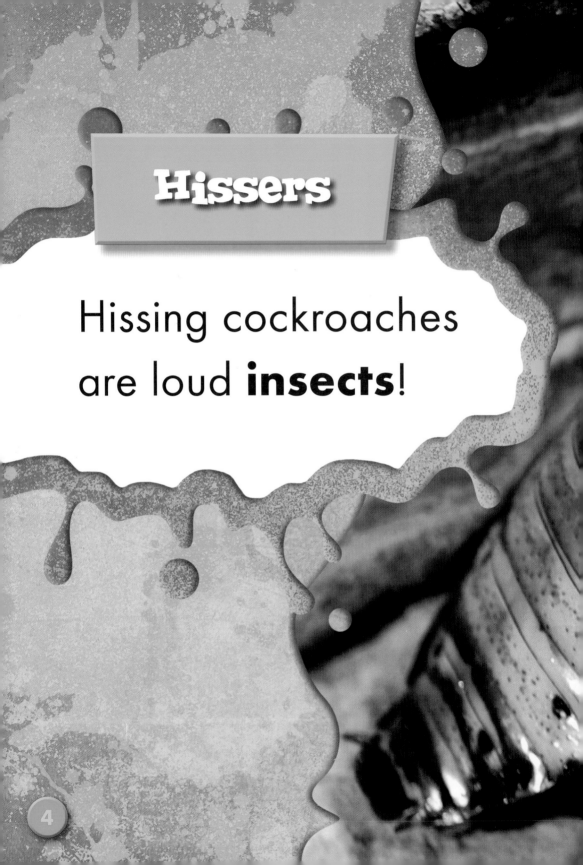

Hissers

Hissing cockroaches are loud **insects**!

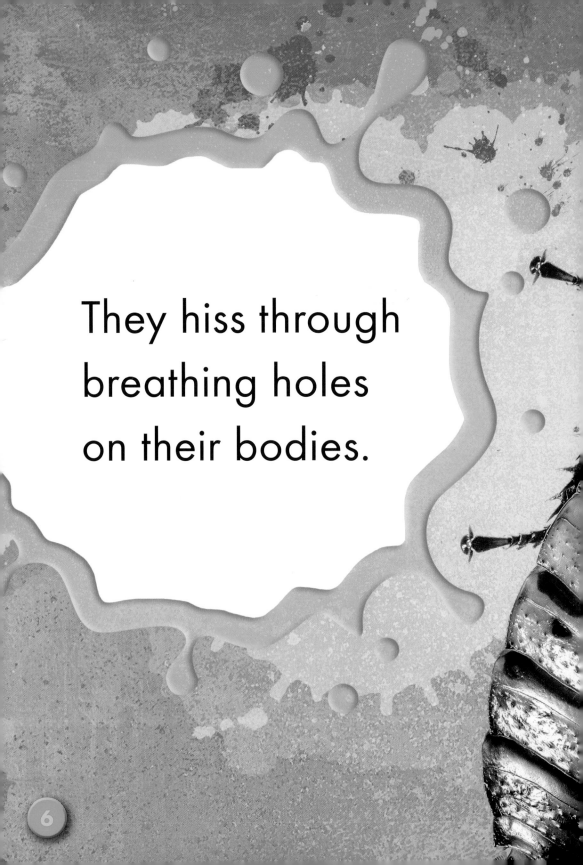

They hiss through breathing holes on their bodies.

breathing holes

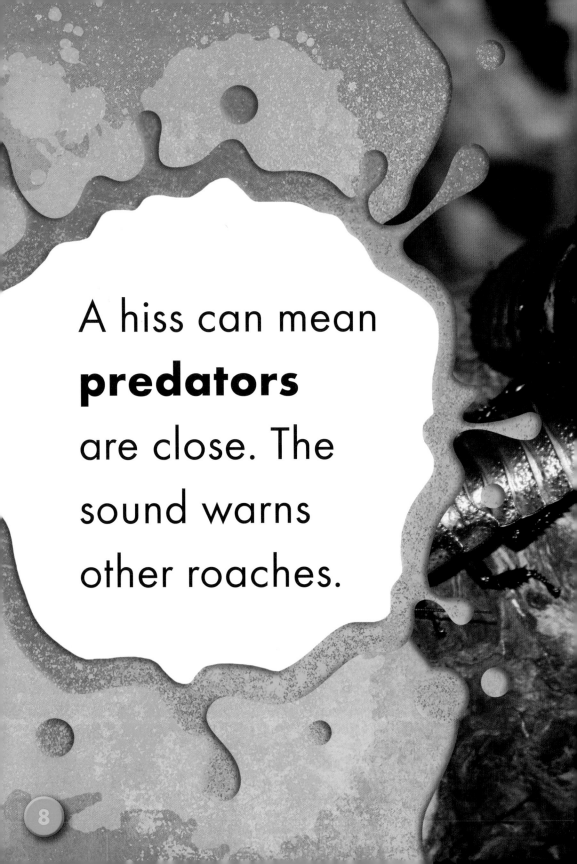

A hiss can mean **predators** are close. The sound warns other roaches.

Fight Time

The noise can
also mean a
fight. Males hiss
at one another!

Males also **ram** their heads to fight. They hit with their **horns**.

In Hiding

Hissing cockroaches often stay under leaves and logs.

They come out
to eat fruits
and leaves.

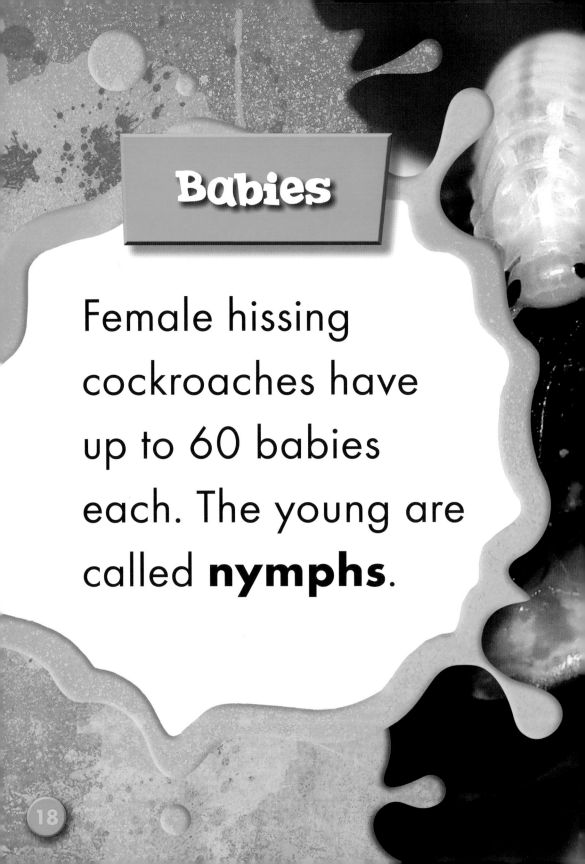

Babies

Female hissing cockroaches have up to 60 babies each. The young are called **nymphs**.

Nymphs **molt** six times as they grow. Then they are adults!

Glossary

horns—hard bumps by the head

insects—small animals with six legs and hard outer bodies; an insect's body is divided into three parts.

molt—to shed skin

nymphs—baby hissing cockroaches

predators—animals that hunt other animals for food

ram—to hit and push hard

To Learn More

AT THE LIBRARY

Amstutz, Lisa J. *Cockroaches.* North Mankato, Minn.: Capstone Press, 2014.

Baughman, Michelle. *A Day in the Life of a Cockroach.* Mustang, Okla.: Tate Publishing, 2009.

Goldish, Meish. *Hungry Cockroaches.* New York, N.Y.: Bearport Pub., 2008.

ON THE WEB

Learning more about hissing cockroaches is as easy as 1, 2, 3.

1. Go to www.factsurfer.com.

2. Enter "hissing cockroaches" into the search box.

3. Click the "Surf" button and you will see a list of related web sites.

With factsurfer.com, finding more information is just a click away.

Index

The images in this book are reproduced through the courtesy of: skydie, front cover; Aleksey Stemmer, pp. 5, 7, 15; Sabena Jane Blackbird/ Alamy, p. 9; Rosa Jay, p. 11 (top); 2happy, p. 11 (bottom); Einar Muoni, p. 13; Hakoar, p. 17; Matt Reinbold/ Flickr, p. 19; NHPA/ SuperStock, p. 21.